HAL•LEONARD

JAZZ PLAY ALONG

Book and CD for B♭, E♭, C and Bass Clef Instruments

volume **62**

Arranged by Mark Taylor
Produced by Paul Murtha

JAZZ-ROCK FUSION
9 favorite tunes

BOOK

TITLE	PAGE NUMBERS			
	C Treble Instruments	B♭ Instruments	E♭ Instruments	C Bass Instruments
Brown Hornet	4	18	32	46
Chameleon	5	19	33	47
Got a Match?	6	20	34	48
Loose Ends	8	22	36	50
Revelation	10	24	38	52
Snakes	12	26	40	54
Spain	14	28	42	56
Three Views of a Secret	16	30	44	58
Watermelon Man	7	21	35	49

CD

TITLE	CD Track Number Split Track / Melody	CD Track Number Full Stereo Track
Brown Hornet	1	2
Chameleon	3	4
Got a Match?	5	6
Loose Ends	7	8
Revelation	9	10
Snakes	11	12
Spain	13	14
Three Views of a Secret	15	16
Watermelon Man	17	18
B♭ Tuning Notes		19

ISBN 978-1-4234-1340-0

HAL•LEONARD®
CORPORATION
7777 W. BLUEMOUND RD. P.O. BOX 13819 MILWAUKEE, WI 53213

Visit Hal Leonard Online at
www.halleonard.com

T0083929

JAZZ-ROCK FUSION

Volume 62

Arranged by Mark Taylor
Produced by Paul Murtha

Featured Players:

Graham Breedlove–Trumpet
John Desalme–Saxophones
Tony Nalker–Piano
Jim Roberts–Bass
Steve Fidyk–Drums

Recorded at Bias Studios, Springfield, Virginia
Bob Dawson, Engineer

HOW TO USE THE CD:

Each song has <u>two</u> tracks:

1) Split Track/Melody

Woodwind, Brass, Keyboard, and **Mallet Players** can use this track as a learning tool for melody style and inflection.

Bass Players can learn and perform with this track – remove the recorded bass track by turning down the volume on the LEFT channel.

Keyboard and **Guitar Players** can learn and perform with this track – remove the recorded piano part by turning down the volume on the RIGHT channel.

2) Full Stereo Track

Soloists or **Groups** can learn and perform with this accompaniment track with the RHYTHM SECTION only.

BROWN HORNET

BY MILES DAVIS

C VERSION   MED. JAZZ ROCK

CHAMELEON

By Herbie Hancock, Paul Jackson,
Harvey Mason and Bennie Maupin

C VERSION

GOT A MATCH?

BY CHICK COREA

WATERMELON MAN

BY HERBIE HANCOCK

LOOSE ENDS

CD
7 : SPLIT TRACK/MELODY
8 : FULL STEREO TRACK

MUSIC BY MICHAEL STERN

C VERSION

REVELATION

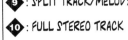

MUSIC BY RUSSELL FERRANTE
AND LORRAINE PERRY

C VERSION

SNAKES

BY MARCUS MILLER

C VERSION

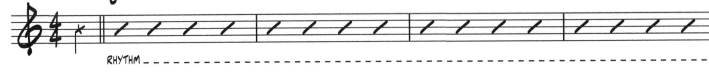

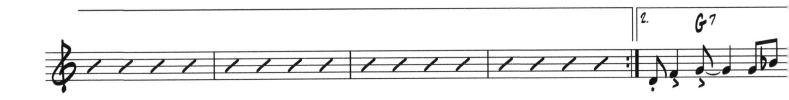

SPAIN

BY CHICK COREA

C VERSION   MED. SAMBA

THREE VIEWS OF A SECRET

BY JACO PASTORIUS

CD
15 : SPLIT TRACK/MELODY
16 : FULL STEREO TRACK

C VERSION

BROWN HORNET

BY MILES DAVIS

CHAMELEON

BY HERBIE HANCOCK, PAUL JACKSON,
HARVEY MASON AND BENNIE MAUPIN

B♭ VERSION

GOT A MATCH?

BY CHICK COREA

WATERMELON MAN

BY HERBIE HANCOCK

Bb VERSION

LOOSE ENDS

MUSIC BY MICHAEL STERN

REVELATION

MUSIC BY RUSSELL FERRANTE
AND LORRAINE PERRY

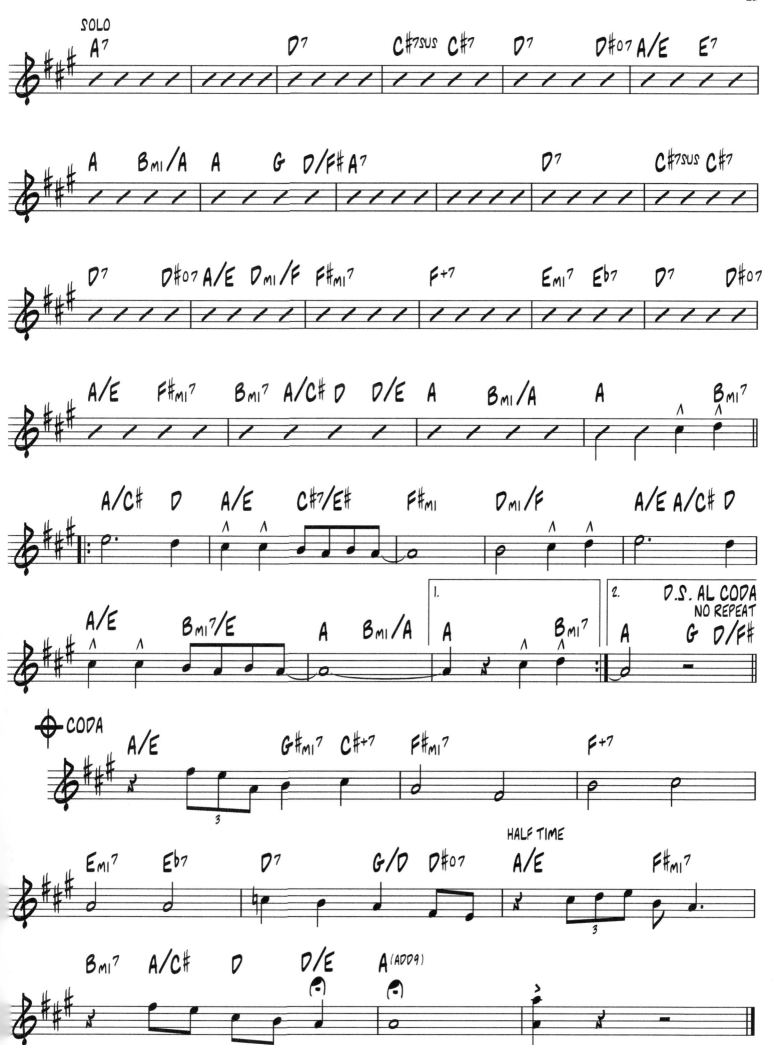

SNAKES

BY MARCUS MILLER

CD

🔟🔟 : SPLIT TRACK/MELODY

🔟🔟 : FULL STEREO TRACK

Bb VERSION

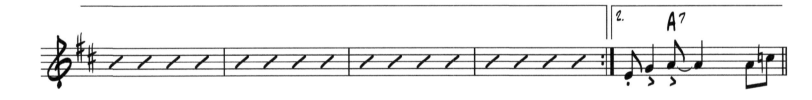

SPAIN

BY CHICK COREA

CD

15 : SPLIT TRACK/MELODY
16 : FULL STEREO TRACK

THREE VIEWS OF A SECRET

BY JACO PASTORIUS

Bb VERSION

BROWN HORNET

BY MILES DAVIS

CHAMELEON

GOT A MATCH?

BY CHICK COREA

WATERMELON MAN

BY HERBIE HANCOCK

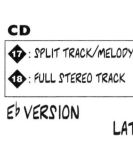

Loose Ends

MUSIC BY MICHAEL STERN

REVELATION

MUSIC BY RUSSELL FERRANTE
AND LORRAINE PERRY

CD
◆ 9 : SPLIT TRACK/MELODY
◆ 10 : FULL STEREO TRACK

E♭ VERSION

SNAKES

BY MARCUS MILLER

CD
11 : SPLIT TRACK/MELODY
12 : FULL STEREO TRACK

Eb VERSION

MED. ROCK

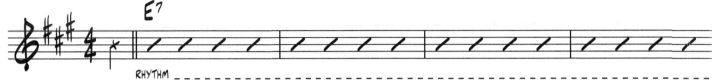

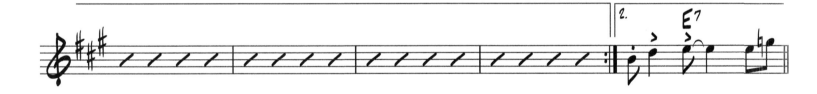

SPAIN

BY CHICK COREA

CD
- 13 : SPLIT TRACK/MELODY
- 14 : FULL STEREO TRACK

E♭ VERSION

MED. SAMBA

43

THREE VIEWS OF A SECRET

BY JACO PASTORIUS

Brown Hornet

BY MILES DAVIS

CHAMELEON

BY HERBIE HANCOCK, PAUL JACKSON,
HARVEY MASON AND BENNIE MAUPIN

GOT A MATCH?

BY CHICK COREA

CD
◆5: SPLIT TRACK/MELODY
◆6: FULL STEREO TRACK

WATERMELON MAN

BY HERBIE HANCOCK

CD
17: SPLIT TRACK/MELODY
18: FULL STEREO TRACK

Loose Ends

MUSIC BY MICHAEL STERN

REVELATION

MUSIC BY RUSSELL FERRANTE
AND LORRAINE PERRY

SNAKES

BY MARCUS MILLER

CD
- 🔷 11 : SPLIT TRACK/MELODY
- 🔷 12 : FULL STEREO TRACK

9: C VERSION
MED. ROCK

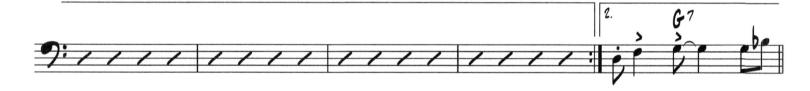

CD
13 : SPLIT TRACK/MELODY
14 : FULL STEREO TRACK

SPAIN

BY CHICK COREA

THREE VIEWS OF A SECRET

BY JACO PASTORIUS

HAL•LEONARD
JAZZ PLAY-ALONG SERIES

HAL•LEONARD®

www.halleonard.com

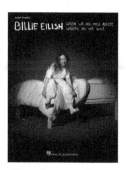     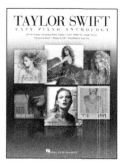

ARTIST TRANSCRIPTIONS®

Artist Transcriptions are authentic, note-for-note transcriptions of today's hottest artists in jazz, pop and rock. These outstanding, accurate arrangements are in an easy-to-read format which includes all essential lines. **Artist Transcriptions** can be used to perform, sequence or for reference.

CLARINET
00672423	Buddy De Franco Collection	$19.95

FLUTE
00672379	Eric Dolphy Collection	$19.95
00672582	The Very Best of James Galway	$19.99
00672372	James Moody Collection – Sax and Flute	$19.95

GUITAR & BASS
00660113	Guitar Style of George Benson	$19.99
00672573	Ray Brown – Legendary Jazz Bassist	$22.99
00672331	Ron Carter Collection	$19.99
00660115	Al Di Meola – Friday Night in San Francisco	$17.99
00604043	Al Di Meola – Music, Words, Pictures	$14.95
00125617	Best of Herb Ellis	$19.99
00673245	Jazz Style of Tal Farlow	$24.99
00699306	Jim Hall – Exploring Jazz Guitar	$19.99
00672353	The Joe Pass Collection	$19.99
00673216	John Patitucci	$17.99
00672374	Johnny Smith – Guitar Solos	$24.99
00672320	Mark Whitfield Guitar Collection	$19.95

PIANO & KEYBOARD
00672338	The Monty Alexander Collection	$19.95
00672487	Monty Alexander Plays Standards	$19.95
00672520	Count Basie Collection	$19.95
00192307	Bebop Piano Legends	$19.99
00113680	Blues Piano Legends	$22.99
00672526	The Bill Charlap Collection	$19.99
00278003	A Charlie Brown Christmas	$17.99
00672439	Cyrus Chestnut Collection	$19.95
00672300	Chick Corea – Paint the World	$19.99
00146105	Bill Evans – Alone	$19.99
00672548	The Mastery of Bill Evans	$16.99
00672425	Bill Evans – Piano Interpretations	$22.99
00672365	Bill Evans – Play Standards	$22.99
00121885	Bill Evans – Time Remembered	$19.99
00672510	Bill Evans Trio Vol. 1: 1959-1961	$27.99
00672511	Bill Evans Trio Vol. 2: 1962-1965	$27.99
00672512	Bill Evans Trio Vol. 3: 1968-1974	$29.99
00672513	Bill Evans Trio Vol. 4: 1979-1980	$24.95
00193332	Erroll Garner – Concert by the Sea	$22.99
00672486	Vince Guaraldi Collection	$19.99
00289644	The Definitive Vince Guaraldi	$34.99
00672419	Herbie Hancock Collection	$22.99
00672438	Hampton Hawes Collection	$19.95
00672322	Ahmad Jamal Collection	$24.99
00255671	Jazz Piano Masterpieces	$19.99
00124367	Jazz Piano Masters Play Rodgers & Hammerstein	$19.99
00672564	Best of Jeff Lorber	$19.99
00672476	Brad Mehldau Collection	$22.99
00672388	Best of Thelonious Monk	$22.99
00672389	Thelonious Monk Collection	$24.99
00672390	Thelonious Monk Plays Jazz Standards – Volume 1	$22.99
00672391	Thelonious Monk Plays Jazz Standards – Volume 2	$22.99
00672433	Jelly Roll Morton – The Piano Rolls	$17.99
00672553	Charlie Parker Piano featuring The Paul Smith Trio (Book/CD)	$19.95
00264094	Oscar Peterson – Night Train	$19.99
00672544	Oscar Peterson – Originals	$14.99
00672531	Oscar Peterson – Plays Duke Ellington	$24.99
00672563	Oscar Peterson – A Royal Wedding Suite	$19.99
00672569	Oscar Peterson – Tracks	$19.99
00672533	Oscar Peterson – Trios	$29.99
00672534	Very Best of Oscar Peterson	$22.95
00672371	Bud Powell Classics	$22.99
00672376	Bud Powell Collection	$24.99
00672507	Gonzalo Rubalcaba Collection	$19.95
00672303	Horace Silver Collection	$24.99
00672316	Art Tatum Collection	$24.99
00672355	Art Tatum Solo Book	$19.99
00672357	The Billy Taylor Collection	$24.95
00673215	McCoy Tyner	$22.99
00672321	Cedar Walton Collection	$19.95
00672519	Kenny Werner Collection	$19.95
00672434	Teddy Wilson Collection	$22.99

SAXOPHONE
00672566	The Mindi Abair Collection	$14.99
00673244	Julian "Cannonball" Adderley Collection	$22.99
00673237	Michael Brecker	$19.99
00672429	Michael Brecker Collection	$24.99
00672394	James Carter Collection	$19.95
00672529	John Coltrane – Giant Steps	$17.99
00672494	John Coltrane – A Love Supreme	$16.99
00672493	John Coltrane Plays "Coltrane Changes"	$19.95
00672453	John Coltrane Plays Standards	$24.99
00673233	John Coltrane Solos	$27.99
00672328	Paul Desmond Collection	$19.99
00672530	Kenny Garrett Collection	$22.99
00699375	Stan Getz	$19.99
00672377	Stan Getz – Bossa Novas	$22.99
00672375	Stan Getz – Standards	$19.99
00673254	Great Tenor Sax Solos	$22.99
00672523	Coleman Hawkins Collection	$22.99
00672330	Best of Joe Henderson	$24.99
00673239	Best of Kenny G	$22.99
00673229	Kenny G – Breathless	$19.99
00672462	Kenny G – Classics in the Key of G	$22.99
00672485	Kenny G – Faith: A Holiday Album	$17.99
00672373	Kenny G – The Moment	$19.99
00672498	Jackie McLean Collection	$19.95
00672372	James Moody Collection – Sax and Flute	$19.95
00672416	Frank Morgan Collection	$19.95
00672539	Gerry Mulligan Collection	$22.99
00672561	Best of Sonny Rollins	$19.95
00102751	Sonny Rollins, Art Blakey & Kenny Drew with the Modern Jazz Quartet	$17.95
00675000	David Sanborn Collection	$19.95
00672528	The Bud Shank Collection	$19.95
00672491	The New Best of Wayne Shorter	$24.99
00672550	The Sonny Stitt Collection	$19.95
00672524	Lester Young Collection	$19.99

TROMBONE
00672332	J.J. Johnson Collection	$22.99
00672489	Steve Turré Collection	$19.99

TRUMPET
00672557	Herb Alpert Collection	$19.99
00672480	Louis Armstrong Collection	$19.99
00672481	Louis Armstrong Plays Standards	$19.99
00672435	Chet Baker Collection	$22.99
00672556	Best of Chris Botti	$19.99
00672448	Miles Davis – Originals, Vol. 1	$19.99
00672451	Miles Davis – Originals, Vol. 2	$19.95
00672449	Miles Davis – Standards, Vol. 2	$19.95
00672479	Dizzy Gillespie Collection	$19.99
00673214	Freddie Hubbard	$19.99
00672506	Chuck Mangione Collection	$19.99
00672525	Arturo Sandoval – Trumpet Evolution	$19.99

JAZZ INSTRUCTION & IMPROVISATION

BOOKS FOR ALL INSTRUMENTS FROM HAL LEONARD

500 JAZZ LICKS
by Brent Vaartstra
This book aims to assist you on your journey to play jazz fluently. These short phrases and ideas we call "licks" will help you understand how to navigate the common chords and chord progressions you will encounter. Adding this vocabulary to your arsenal will send you down the right path and improve your jazz playing, regardless of your instrument.
00142384 ....$16.99

1001 JAZZ LICKS
by Jack Shneidman
Cherry Lane Music
This book presents 1,001 melodic gems played over dozens of the most important chord progressions heard in jazz. This is the ideal book for beginners seeking a well-organized, easy-to-follow encyclopedia of jazz vocabulary, as well as professionals who want to take their knowledge of the jazz language to new heights.
02500133 ....$14.99

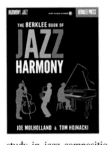

THE BERKLEE BOOK OF JAZZ HARMONY
by Joe Mulholland & Tom Hojnacki
Learn jazz harmony, as taught at Berklee College of Music. This text provides a strong foundation in harmonic principles, supporting further study in jazz composition, arranging, and improvisation. It covers basic chord types and their tensions, with practical demonstrations of how they are used in characteristic jazz contexts and an accompanying recording that lets you hear how they can be applied.
00113755 Book/Online Audio....................$19.99

BUILDING A JAZZ VOCABULARY
By Mike Steinel
A valuable resource for learning the basics of jazz from Mike Steinel of the University of North Texas. It covers: the basics of jazz • how to build effective solos • a comprehensive practice routine • and a jazz vocabulary of the masters.
00849911 ....$19.99

COMPREHENSIVE TECHNIQUE FOR JAZZ MUSICIANS
2ND EDITION
by Bert Ligon
Houston Publishing
An incredible presentation of the most practical exercises an aspiring jazz student could want. All are logically interwoven with fine "real world" examples from jazz to classical. This book is an essential anthology of technical, compositional, and theoretical exercises, with lots of musical examples.
00030455 ....$34.99

EAR TRAINING
by Keith Wyatt, Carl Schroeder and Joe Elliott
Musicians Institute Press
Covers: basic pitch matching • singing major and minor scales • identifying intervals • transcribing melodies and rhythm • identifying chords and progressions • seventh chords and the blues • modal interchange, chromaticism, modulation • and more.
00695198 Book/Online Audio....................$24.99

EXERCISES AND ETUDES FOR THE JAZZ INSTRUMENTALIST
by J.J. Johnson
Designed as study material and playable by any instrument, these pieces run the gamut of the jazz experience, featuring common and uncommon time signatures and keys, and styles from ballads to funk. They are progressively graded so that both beginners and professionals will be challenged by the demands of this wonderful music.
00842018 Bass Clef Edition $19.99
00842042 Treble Clef Edition $16.95

HOW TO PLAY FROM A REAL BOOK
by Robert Rawlins
Explore, understand, and perform the songs in real books with the techniques in this book. Learn how to analyze the form and harmonic structure, insert an introduction, interpret the melody, improvise on the chords, construct bass lines, voice the chords, add substitutions, and more. It addresses many aspects of solo and small band performance that can improve your own playing and your understanding of what others are doing around you.
00312097 ....$19.99

JAZZ DUETS
ETUDES FOR PHRASING AND ARTICULATION
by Richard Lowell
Berklee Press
With these 27 duets in jazz and jazz-influenced styles, you will learn how to improve your ear, sense of timing, phrasing, and your facility in bringing theoretical principles into musical expression. Covers: jazz staccato & legato • scales, modes & harmonies • phrasing within and between measures • swing feel • and more.
00302151 ....$14.99

JAZZ THEORY & WORKBOOK
by Lilian Dericq & Étienne Guéreau
Designed for all instrumentalists, this book teaches how jazz standards are constructed. It is also a great resource for arrangers and composers seeking new writing tools. While some of the musical examples are pianistic, this book is not exclusively for keyboard players.
00159022 ....$19.99

JAZZ THEORY RESOURCES
by Bert Ligon
Houston Publishing, Inc.
This is a jazz theory text in two volumes. **Volume 1 includes**: review of basic theory • rhythm in jazz performance • triadic generalization • diatonic harmonic progressions and analysis • substitutions and turnarounds • and more. **Volume 2 includes**: modes and modal frameworks • quartal harmony • extended tertian structures and triadic superimposition • pentatonic applications • coloring "outside" the lines and beyond • and more.
00030458 Volume 1 ....$39.99
00030459 Volume 2 ....$32.99

JAZZOLOGY
THE ENCYCLOPEDIA OF JAZZ THEORY FOR ALL MUSICIANS
by Robert Rawlins and Nor Eddine Bahha
This comprehensive resource covers a variety of jazz topics, for beginners and pros of any instrument. The book serves as an encyclopedia for reference, a thorough methodology for the student, and a workbook for the classroom.
00311167 ....$24.99

MODALOGY
SCALES, MODES & CHORDS: THE PRIMORDIAL BUILDING BLOCKS OF MUSIC
by Jeff Brent with Schell Barkley
Primarily a music theory reference, this book presents a unique perspective on the origins, interlocking aspects, and usage of the most common scales and modes in occidental music. Anyone wishing to seriously explore the realms of scales, modes, and their real-world functions will find the most important issues dealt with in meticulous detail within these pages.
00312274 ....$24.99

THE SOURCE
THE DICTIONARY OF CONTEMPORARY AND TRADITIONAL SCALES
by Steve Barta
This book serves as an informative guide for people who are looking for good, solid information regarding scales, chords, and how they work together. It provides right and left hand fingerings for scales, chords, and complete inversions. Includes over 20 different scales, each written in all 12 keys.
00240885 ....$19.99

HAL•LEONARD®
www.halleonard.com

Prices, contents & availability subject to change without notice.

0421
068